D1520241

Flux & Reflux

Flux &
Reflux

Journies in a Magical Fluid

Douglas Blazek

oyez berkeley
1970

Some of these poems have previously appeared in:

Arts in Society
Broken Cobwebs
Chelsea
Christmas 1968
The Far Point
The Human Voice
Kayak
Lillabulero
The Malahat Review
Meatball
New: American & Canadian Poetry
The New Generation Anthology
The Orange Bear Reader
Quetzal
Wascana Review
Wormwood Review

The cover illustration is by Michael Myers.

For Kel

who would laugh at my dedicating
a book to him or for even writing one.
And he's right! I wouldn't have
done it if the curtain hadn't of
caught me each time it came down.

"The trouble with literacy is
that it enables you to predict
which side to be on which means
you are pre-dicted
before anything happens."

— Ed Dorn

FOR THOSE ADVANCED ENOUGH TO LOVE

"What have I made of living
but to reach for life."
   — Edouard Maunick

All that I have
to celebrate
is in the kitchen
where I have learned
the plot of my life —

Knives of airplane wings
forks of mathematics
spoons of conversation

Shipwrecks of cereal boxes
swamps of mason jar jelly
rainstorms of kool aid

It is magic,
my life reached for
and placed before me —
the details of Christmas
are everywhere

Kitchen poetry, daily love
for those most advanced
in perception and celebration.

CALENDARS DISSOLVED IN NEUROTIC ACID

A little sparrow
hangs in the tree like a rag

Staring at the sun
wondering where to go

No traffic behind
pushing him on

I run some water
in the sink

Someone is always
running water

If not running water
they're moving furniture

Constantly
they know what to do

Strange I never see them
staring at the sun.

WHAT WE HAVE IN THE WANTING

A stone
has more hours
than we,
the wind
more muscles
but neither
more dreams —
the ceremony
of the oceans
is the ceremony
of the wheel,
and the planet's
ritual of noise
revolves into
silence at its
highest peak
and it's all as
handy as a miracle.

THE MIND'S ALWAYS GOIN' WEST

—for Alta

We couldn't look at each other
as Woody sang "This Land is Your Land,
this Land is My Land"

The phonograph spinning his voice
the day after he died

We were crying, the
unofficial national anthem
threaded into our tears
as deep as the long green grass
we crossed coming west

Woody beginning to rot
as we sifted through his words
for the handle — it
was there, Woody
always left a handle: you and me,

This land was made for you and me.

THE SIGNATURE OF MYSTERIES
IN THE UNIVERSE

    Having an understanding
sense of order
    of how things are forced together
by unknown winds
    I don't worry much about
the spots on my bed —
    a little Rorschach of tar,
a re-creation of the solar system
    by one of my favorite
       leaky pens
and the far remains of a
    grapevine spilled from a
       metal glass —
The entire system of things
    is mirrored on this sheet
and the scratches on my
       headboard
  are caused by my fingers
    which can't seem to
engrain themselves deep enough
    even in the simplest of things.

A SOFT BREVITY

From a thought of what I am
to the insect bones of an ash-withered sparrow
to centuries of puddled gum wrappers
to fence posts nesting crippled lilacs
to curtains whispering to window sills
to porches drinking soft rockers
to the trees foaming in air
to candles arching paraffin eyelids
to thick air swimming by my full body
and sunlight skipping like a young boy
across the planet.

WAITING FOR THINGS TO BECOME
AS THEY ARE

Who is responsible
for the awkward torture
captured in my sleep

Responsible for making
everything too possible

The predictions of tragedy
and no bulletproof philosophy

This fringe panic magnificence
with cars hooding perfect
screams of baffled angels

Who is responsible
for the dust
of a far off reality

And the immediate storm of waiting.

EARTH SPROCKET

Along the ocean
birds dash off miles
of foreign language
punctuated by driftwood
and dixie cups.

The funny tracks
disappear at high tide —
a sandy magazine is
swept into a murky window.

In the air the
language-makers applaud,
in the ocean
old tricks are smoothed out.

The sand sleeps all
the time — this sandclock
does not pour — it
possesses all time and
goes no where.

Clouds keep pantomiming
the movement of earth.
they are getting dingy and
need washing.

Going home, streetcars
drive through bathrooms of rain.
a gray elephant is giving
birth to the entire ocean!

We pass doorways of mood,
streets that duck away and
hide in gloom.

Inside my room the
afternoon passes without breathing.

A second before dusk the
room widens with the sun's breath.
moisture expands back to invisibility.

Flowers open their shirts.

It is the last moment of recess,
the last moment of freedom —
the room prepares to narrow again
and the sun, slipped through the
blinds like shredded cole slaw,
is about to force everything
into seriousness.

Imprisoned by thought
darkness sneaks up behind me —
the ocean rides and rides,
the birds are busy again
giving us something to translate.

THE DOOR MY HAND REMEMBERS
IS HANDLELESS

Flakes of ceiling skin
cellophane sun oiling a universe
of charm bracelet people
crankcase streets
papers slap around by the curb
a gray Volkswagen grinds up the hill
with a green canoe on its back
and a white Ford with a crinkled side
slips around the corner like a fish
and slides down the hill, both drivers
going to their dandruffed homes of
greasy windows, girdles stuffed in corners
spider threads waving from cornices
hair clogged in bathroom drains
smells of sewing machines and straight pins.
O revolution! go hang yourself!

A WANDERING SHIMMERED TOUCH

Who follows us home
each night
and wraps up our kiss?

Who lives inside the trees
that drowns
running to our feet?

Who listens when sidewalks
cling to our eyes
and fall heavy
as we close our door
with all the noise
of the universe?

Is there anyone
who knows the gift
that floats to us
as we awake
and can open it
so as not to disturb
the trance of sun?

A GUIDED TOUR OF THE NIGHT

Lemonade stands
being taken in
cars softly going to sleep
in garages
their crankcases
dripping black sperm
the sun tumbling
over the foot of the horizon
stars being threaded
into the sky
as the night sinks
into the mattress earth.

Somewhere swollen rivers
are yawning
and another young girl is gone.

Somewhere in New York an
old woman holds a sign
saying "Bomb Hanoi"
but nobody is holding
up a sign reading
"Bomb New York"
how can anyone build
a bomb or hold a sign
after Hiroshima?

The universe is silent
preparing for
its Last Supper . . .

Crying, they say, makes
the ribs grow lean —
it is winter and the trees
look unusually thin to me.

THE VICIOUS ROBBERY

I was with James
walking down Evergreen
just off Wells
coming home through
a pre-sun mist
when this juiced old man
leans into us
waving a knife that looked
duller than liver sausage.

He wanted our money
or our lives and
we had little of either
but obviously more than he.

His eyes were slipping
and the knife kept drooping
like a hardon he didn't want.

Between us we gathered
two dollars and sixty three cents
and wondered how long that
would sustain him.

The sadness of defeat
without a battle — the
loss of every dream and,
finally, the ability to dream.

He stumbled away
bruising the fog looking
for the end of the street
and someone who won't
knock him senseless
when he repeats the night over.

TECHNOLOGY

For years
a little bird
had
been
nesting
outside my window
in
a silver leaf maple.

Sometime
ago
he died
and
for weeks
I
have been watching
him
rot.

Today
I noticed
that
all of his
skin
was
gone
and I could see
his
insides
which
were made of

springs
and various
cog wheels.

I could see
a mainspring
with
a
turnkey
which
I
wound.

Upon winding
I held
the bird
in
my hands
and flung
it
into the air
to
which
it
took
as
before.

As I
turned my back
to go in
I
could see

it
was heading
toward
the
sun
on which
I
could see
if
I
squinted
hard enough
a
little
turnkey. . .

LUBRICATION

The ocean does not hold still
it is a paranoid junkie
that keeps hiding its stash
but sitting here
my eyes the velocity of water
I cannot tell
that there are any secrets
I am only told by biologists
and mystics and microfilm of
downed ships and men drowned.
it's the usual thing one hears
about and I suppose that if one
views the ocean enough it gets
to be the same thing much
like getting up in the morning
and trying to find a matching
pair of socks in the top dresser
drawer or a mortician tying
tags around toes —

The ocean is not a polio victim
its icebergs and glaciers are skull caps.
the ocean is my brain —
it is the shore where
my body is,   on the sand
my hands grab onto things.
the ocean is my brain.
it cannot grab onto anything
not even its own slippery self.
it is a lubricant — but what does it oil?

FUNCTIONING

Today is Wednesday
I stare at the lightbulbs
on the ceiling.

Today is Thursday
I stare at the lightbulbs
on the ceiling.

Today is Friday
I stare at the lightbulbs
on the ceiling.

Saturday
the same.

Sunday
as well.

Sometimes there are five.
when I stare long
there are sometimes six
or longer
only four.

Today is Monday
I stare at the lightbulbs
on the ceiling.
there are five.

Today is Tuesday
I stare at the lightbulbs
on the ceiling.
there are five.

I keep proving
to myself
over and over again
things I know.

SIGHT OF HAND

The hand is magical
held before me —

I move fingers
wrist
thumb kisses palm

Push away something
point at something
touch something
grasp something
say fuck you

And I'm told my nails
keep growing
after I die.

THE TOY GUN OF MY CHILDREN

The woman
with moonbelly
poses for hope.

The tin plaything, a shape
used in destroying gymshoes
ends up mass produced
for those whose hate drools
when dirt clogs aortas.

The Brain
speaks in our flesh.

Flesh
becomes the shape
of all weapons.

The woman
with moonbelly
poses for hope, it
is a drawing
        not
from a holster
but from the heart
where all flesh
finally gathers.

A CELLULAR SONG

—for baby Molly

One keeps saying
the same thing
over and over
a little different each time
until
it is the complete opposite.

There is the solar system
in my neighborhood:
Jupiter Street, Saturn Street,
Mars . . .

We take a bath
on Saturday
stepping out of the tub
with smooth moonflesh.

It all happens this way, Molly,
something is seen
something is done
and after awhile we
know it so well
it becomes something different
each time.

The world
is as young as you are —
your body will grow
but your cells will
remain the same size.

The water in the tub
drains under the solar system
in unopened veins, but
we saw it once
coming out of the faucet
splashed in it
and we will see it again
as the ocean
or when it rains.

The neighborhood will grow
our smooth flesh will crinkle
things will gurgle
down the drain
and reappear as something else
but
cells remain the same size.

AGE IS A USELESS THING

Expending my time
by the ocean
as it expends all
        time
    uses it out of existence
the way we do
        as we get older.

Along the shore
a brown dog
    running its freedom
a young man
    unstringing his legs.

Time is as old
    as it always was
and the ocean as young
    as it always will.

Age is a useless thing,
    unless you're human
        and old
    and can't run anymore.

BY THE SKIN OF DAYS

Somehow
the shoes will hold together
another month
and the chair won't fall apart —
the walls flex shyly as a bus
snorts up the hill like a green animal.

Outside
a girl is walking
dressed in candy wrappers that
have been peeked into.
her breasts move like puppies.

A beach of dust covers the furniture
and the window's mucus saddens
the sky's gray lumber. no
sun crudely burns holes in the sky
nor any hothouse joy,
just a comedy with no laughter,
just the promise of a
raggy soliloquy of beer and
a continuation of the continuation.

AN UNDERSTANDING BEYOND
EXPERIENCE

She was curled up
on the couch
like a weight on a bellbar
tight
snug
complete
her nylons fitted
so perfect
like roadsigns
advertizing Catholic churches.

Beyond her skirt
was a tunnel so
helplessly open
packed with slithery humus
and ruby stalactites.

She was a sleeping
Japanese paper flower
waiting for the fluid
to open her petals —
it was sad
her need to continue
her only life.

I left her there
untouched
knowing I could
have kept my cock
inside her
all night long
like a bookmark.

She was already
had; I shoot
at heavier things.

CALLIGRAPHY OF THE
GRAVE / OUR FINGERPRINTS

When
we first moved here
there were rats in the garage
where the chickens used to be —
small rat-turds littered the floor
like brittle licorice from a berserk machine,
boxes were gnawed by scrofulous
ripsaws and the gymnasium of
paint cans and cracked flower pots was
totally deranged.

A
cat I got from
a jazz piano man skinnier than
a saloon door gave eviction notices
to each rat one by one
until the garage was nothing but a
memory of scurring and gnawing and crapping.
I know there is something bigger
than cats for us —
we all serve a
term as executioner — we leave
our fingerprints on everything .

THE GETTING TO BE POEM

I want a banana the color of my skin
I want a woman to be my skin
I want her sucking that banana
I want the sucking to become peaceful cows
I want the cows to be brown
I want them to be the color of my room
I want my skin to be brown the color of cows
I want my skin to suck peacefulness
I want a woman to be my skin

My walls are brown
my woman is soft
there is peacefulness
I am my room.

THE SUN LISTENING
IN ANOTHER ROOM

Walking eyes
broken eyes
talking wounds.

Exhibition in black
night rustling
frustrated
a dog with no tongue
trying to bark.

Cricket clouds rushing
softly into wounds
women pulling horses
through their birth
talking stars gathering
beyond moons
descending
descending
folding into brilliance
that only blood knows.

SITTING IN MY ROOM
CLUTCHING AT THE
POTENTIALS OF EVERYTHING

Silence is intimate
in this room
the museum made mad
by collecting perfectly
impractical objects
that serve the eye
and taunt with questions.

Silence is a monologue
here
aware of participation
in junk;
unique the sieve that
strains poetry from junk.

Silence is pure freedom
and is abused
when junk becomes transparent
and the smooth forever days
only clutch more of it to
cover death.

Silence contains all activity —
a child studies a war helmet.

BUENA VISTA PARK

Cathedral of willow silence,
fir needles caught in the wind's throat.

Sun mobbing soft twig bones.

Architecture of collapse.
brown blurs
nuzzling green dresses, quivering.

Drowse of the calmest breath.

Weed stalks praying
with nodded heads.

I am the only storm.

VOYAGE OF PRESENCE

the design a stone makes in water
is the very body
I hold together
as waves pull past
playing badminton
and suns of another day
tatter and fade
my body extending outwards
until it becomes the tide
and the drowsy battering of time
absorbs me totally
into its presence.

UNCLOGGED DILEMMA

Leaving for work
this morning
I heard a
crow —
the matches
which I lit
my cigarette
with
said
"Don't Stay Deaf!"

I listened again
for the crow
but heard nothing.

At work
they have
signs
telling us
to T H I N K .

After pouring
my hemoglobin
into the machines
I left for home
where my wife
told me
"Cheer up —
now you're free
to be
yourself again!"

The crows
were still
outside.

The matches
still
in my pocket.

My back
told me
I
wanted
to sleep
but
all I could
think about
was
how to get
my blood back.

Now I know
why they have
those signs
at work!

THE SAYINGS DONATED AND BLOWN

To tell you something new
the trellis of air has
fine trees sprouting from
a vital organ in the solar system.

To tell you something new
the flowerbed is wedged
in the corner of my eye
and has a vicious speed.

To tell you something new
rocks embrace the topsoil
in love and as helpless
as the cracks in the sidewalk.

To tell you something new
topsoil dances to the spade
as a remembrance is smothered
slowly slowly in my mind.

To tell you something new
would be impossible
even if I fed you the world backwards
or threw it on the floor like a dish.

To tell you something new
just for the record
is to play the record again.

FREEDOM IS TAUGHT BEST IN PRISONS

How many men
are in me
                dead?
how many fires
teach me
                nakedness
how many winters
catch me
                still exploring
        the first snowflake?
why has a woman
built
        a brick spider web
        that has trapped me
                processing my days
        like traffic tickets?
what direction
does a man go
        once the door slams
but inward.

DEATH MAKES IT ALL IMPOSSIBLE

Earth would be a nice place
without things dying.

Just can't get used to
animals skinned like plums
in slaughter houses or
raped of life in the field or
mangled in the meat grinder
of automobiles.

And birds dropping out of the sky
and butterflies scooped into nets
and human beings charred
by men on a picnic from morals
shot by men who are children
bombed by men who never could be children
human beings who just die
and hollow-out those who loved them.

Yes, earth would be a nice place
if somehow I could walk inside myself
while death walked outside.

THE CRITICS

I make light bulbs.

Oh, not the ordinary ones
but special ones
yep
the kind that glow forever
the kind that the sun
uses to see where it's going
But

once 'n a while
these guys come by
and tell me
I'm not making 'em right,
need to twist the filaments
a bit more
or sumthin'

There's ways to do it
and there's ways not to

I listen patiently
and
twist the filaments a little —

The sun still finds its way.

IN TIME, INN

Light a candle
let us conceal darkness
put on a record
let us color silence
come to bed
let us find
what is missing
in what we've done
today.

THE AIR OF TOMORROW IS MOLASSES

I could hear her
rattling around her pink
across the courtyard
as unnoted as the rust
around the bathtub drain
me pondering my outdatedness
centuries from now when
computers will be antiques
and men will read us perfunctorily
as we read the Greeks
and this language that fits
my mouth well will sound funny —
ah, but we sat at kitchen tables
and rattled around our pink
and whored ourselves for bits of candy
and died like rats biting air
time having found a place to store us,
the dust piling on as sure as the wars coming.

UNDERGROUND CONSTRUCTION

The air in a coffin
where thunder is solid,
soil deafening for the ear
to touch, rises for lungs to ignite.

What occured the cherry pie guts?
we know the bones quarrel
with their pointless justice —
all they ever did.

Now caught under a mound, the
little rivit precious
holds the structure together.

Shivering cries
trapped beneath the earth
are heard for thousands of years —
patterns rearranging new boundaries.

ODE (yes that's right) TO MY TOOTHBRUSH

Lounging on a shelf
in the medicine cabinet
is my toothbrush streamlined
in a yellow plastic negligee
cuddling next to a rectum of toothpaste
doubled up with cramps.

That toothbrush is
in there doing its stuff
every morning
every evening
as faithful as Lou Gehrig
as caring as a good woman.

And now that I've
compared my toothbrush
to a good woman you expect
me to compare brushing my teeth
to fornicating or something even
more profound (if there is anything)
— but a toothbrush is just a toothbrush
picking out bits of cow,
a lonely thing in a cabinet
making me so attached to it
because of its simple and inevitable function
because of its yellow sadness
because it *can't* be compared to the world.

THE PARTING GLASS

*— for Larry and, of course,
The Clancy Brothers*

After we drank
all the beer
even the warm beer
just to make sure
we didn't
leave a single can
undrunk
I
gathered them
into my arms
those
spent hulks of
tin firewood
and delicately
placed
them into the
garbage.

I am sure
that
all the things
that were
felt
in a lifetime
of being
together
were not
expressed

but
at least
the beer
was drunk
and we had said
goodbye
a little less
sorrowfully.

*Designed & printed by Clifford Burke
at Cranium Press, San Francisco, in
an edition of 1000 copies. July 1970.
Set in linotype Aldus by Holbrook Teter.*